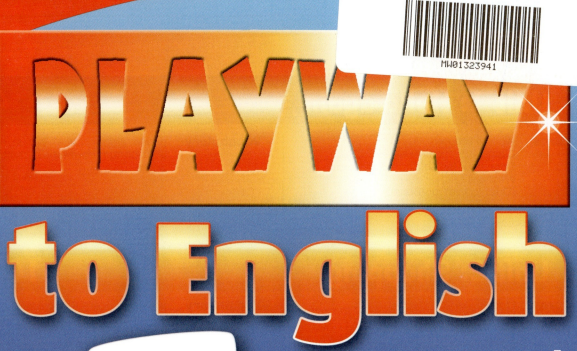

Second edition

2

Pupil's Book

Günter Gerngross • Herbert Puchta

Contents

Unit 1: Hello again — 4-9

Structures
Walk to school.
Close your eyes.
Open your mouth.
What is it?
(One) (apple) for (Benny).

Vocabulary
peach, grapes, nut(s), kiwi(s), strawberry (strawberries), melon
some

Unit 2: Shopping — 10-15

Structures
I (don't) like …
How much is it?
£(2), please.
Goodbye.

Vocabulary
potato(es), carrot(s), onion(s), tomato(es), cucumber(s), red/green pepper(s)

Units 1-2: Show what you can do — 16-17

Unit 3: In my house — 18-23

Structures
In my room there's a (pink) (sofa).
There are (green) (curtains).
That's strange.
Jump down.
Open the (cupboard).
It's my/your turn.
(Three) plus/minus (two) is ….

Vocabulary
curtains, lamp, cupboard, telephone, sofa, chair, table, mat, TV
eleven, twelve, thirteen, fourteen, fifteen, sixteen, seventeen, eighteen, nineteen, twenty

Unit 4: My body — 24-29

Structures
Clap your hands.
Shake your hands/head.
Stamp your feet.
Touch (the chair).
My/Your (shoulder) hurts.
My/Your (feet) hurt.

Vocabulary
hand, mouth, head, ear, eye, nose, arm, tooth/teeth, shoulder, finger, knee, foot/feet, leg, toe(s), tummy

Units 3-4: Show what you can do — 30-31

Unit 5: Clothes — 32-37

Structures
Look at me.
My (jacket) is (green).
My (jeans) are (blue).
(Joe), this (hat) is for you.
I hate it.
Bye-bye.
What a lovely hat!
Stupid me!

Vocabulary
pullover, woolly hat, jeans, skirt, dress, socks, jacket, trainers, T-shirt, hat, cap, shoes
fox
wonderful

Unit 6: Let's count — 38–43

Structures	Vocabulary
I can't do it. Well done! I'm sorry. Throw the dice. I'm/You're the winner.	thirty, forty, fifty, sixty, seventy, eighty, ninety, a/one hundred piggy bank

Units 5–6: Show what you can do — 44–45

Unit 7: Family — 46–51

Structures	Vocabulary
I think (Tom's) family is number (one). In my family there's my (mum). This is my family. The (beaver) is (very) happy. Happy birthday! Do you like (pink roses)? They smell wonderful.	mum, dad, brother, sister, grandpa, grandma racoon, beaver

Unit 8: On the farm — 52–57

Structures	Vocabulary
Who are you?	cow, sheep, horse, pig, duck, cat dog, mouse, hen, earthworm chick

Units 7–8: Show what you can do — 58–59

Unit 9: Travelling — 60–65

Structures	Vocabulary
How do you get to school? By (bus). I walk. (Timmy) goes by (bike). First by (car) and then by (train).	left, right underground, train, car, plane, bus

Unit 10: Holidays — 66–71

Structures	Vocabulary
Let's be quiet. It's asleep. See you again!	cool off lake beach

Units 9–10: Show what you can do — 72–73

Picture Dictionary — 74–80

Unit 1  Hello again

1   **Listen and point. Sing the song.**

2   **Watch the story. Listen and write the numbers.**

Unit 1

3 **Listen and point. Write the numbers.**

Walk to school.   Take out a banana.   Throw the skin away.   Walk on.

4  **Listen and draw.**

5  **Say.**

Close your eyes.　Open your mouth.　What is it?　A (peach).

Unit 1

6 🎧 11 CD 1 **Listen and write the numbers.**

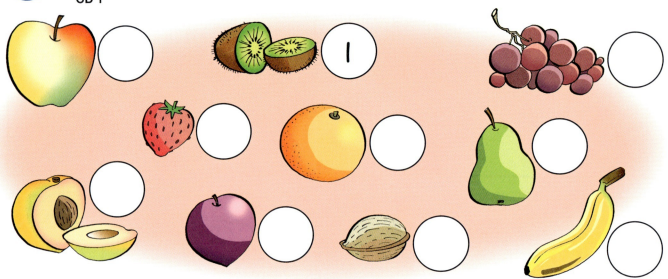

7 🎧 12 CD 1 **Listen and draw. Find the pattern.**

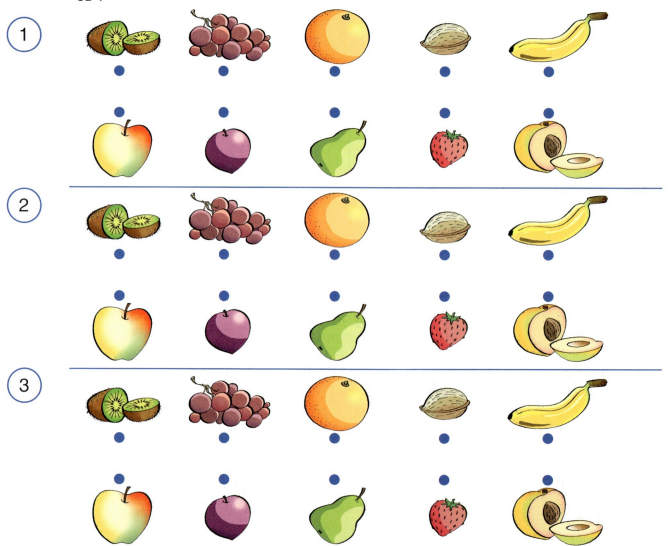

grapes   nut(s)   kiwi(s)   strawberry (strawberries)

8 Listen and read.

1 for Benny,
1 for Linda,
1 for Li
And some for me.

1 for Benny,
2 for Linda,
3 for Li
And 10  for me.

9 Create your own poem.

____ for Benny,

____ for Linda,

____ for Li

And ____ for me.

(One) (apple) for (Benny) and some (grapes) for me.

Unit 2 — Shopping

1 17/18 CD 1 **Listen and point. Say the chant.**

 potatoes

 carrots

 onions

 tomatoes

 cucumbers

 green/red peppers

potato(es)   carrot(s)   onion(s)   tomato(es)   cucumber(s)   red/green pepper(s)

10

Unit 2

2   Listen and write the numbers.

Unit 2

3 Stick and say.

I like ...

I don't like ...

I like ... .   I don't like ... .

Unit 2

4   Watch the story. Listen and stick.

Good morning.   How much is it?   £2, please.   Goodbye.

5   **Listen and point. Act out.**

Unit 2

6 How to make a fruit salad.

You need:
- bowl
- knife
- spoon
- cutting board
- apple
- banana
- some grapes
- kiwi
- some strawberries
- some yoghurt

1 Cut the apple.

2 Cut the banana and some grapes.

3 Cut the kiwi and the strawberries.

4 Add yoghurt.

5 Mix everything.

6 Yummy!

15

Units 1-2

Show what you can do

1 🎧 24 CD 1 **Listen and write the numbers.**

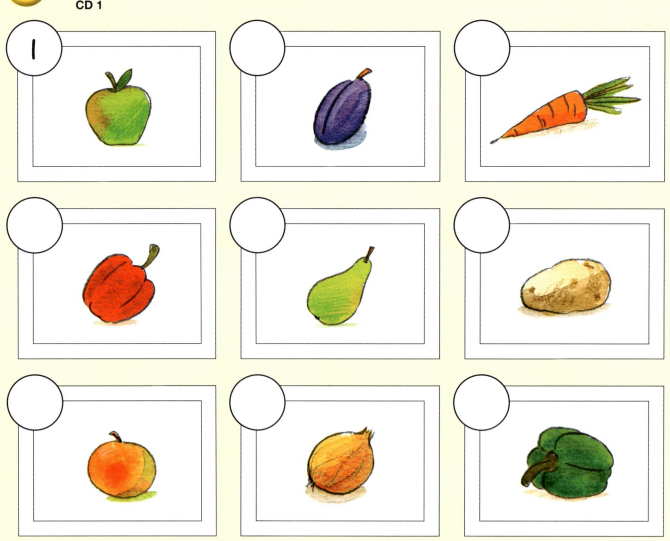

2 **Match the words to the pictures.**

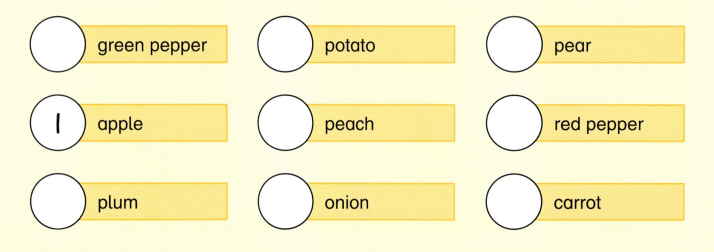

16

Units 1-2

3 Listen and write the numbers.

4 Match the sentences to the pictures.

1	Close your eyes.		Here you are.
	I don't like peppers.		I like carrots.

Unit 3 — In my house

1 🎵 CD 1, 26 — **Listen and point.**

2 🎵 CD 1, 27/28 — **Listen and point. Sing the song.**

curtains   lamp   cupboard   telephone   sofa   chair   table   mat   TV

18

Unit 3

3 🔊 CD 1 29 **Listen and read.**

In my room there's a 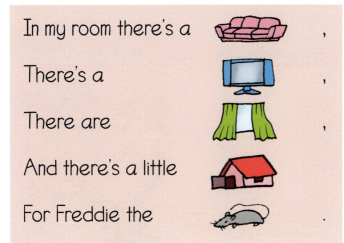 ,
There's a ,
There are ,
And there's a little
For Freddie the .

In my room there's a 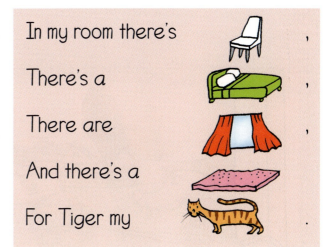 ,
There's a ,
There are ,
And there's a
For Tiger my .

4 🔊 CD 1 30 **Create your own poem.**

WORD PLAY

In my room there's a ⬜ ,

There's a ⬜ ,

There are ⬜ ,

And there's a ⬜

For _____ the ⬜ .

In my room there's a (pink) (sofa)/there are (green) (curtains).

Unit 3

5   **Watch the story. Listen and stick.**

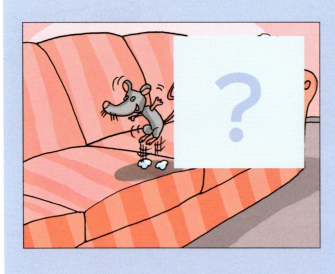
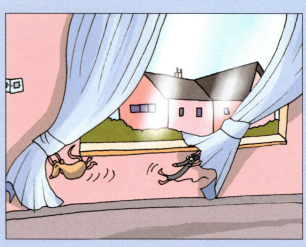

The (sofa) (is) for me and (Fred). All right. Let's watch TV! The've got a cat! Let's run! That's strange. I can smell mice!

Unit 3

6 🎧 CD 1 · 34 **Listen and point. Write the numbers.**

Open the (cupboard).   Climb onto a chair.   Jump down.   You drop the chocolate bar.
Your dog grabs the chocolate bar.   Shout, 'Give it back!'.

7   **Do sums.**

eleven   twelve   thirteen   fourteen   fifteen   sixteen   seventeen   eighteen   nineteen   twenty
(Three) minus/plus (two) is … .   It's my/your turn.

Unit 4 — My body

1  **Listen and write the numbers.**

2 **Play the game. Point and say.**

Nose.

hand   mouth   head   ear   eye   nose   tooth/teeth   shoulder   arm   finger   knee   foot/feet   leg   toe

3   Listen and point. Say the chant.

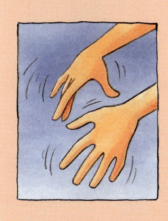

Clap your hands.　Shake your (head).　Stamp your feet.　Touch (the chair).

Unit 4

  Listen and point. Write the numbers.

(Wilbur) runs into the bathroom.

5   Watch the story. Listen and write the numbers.

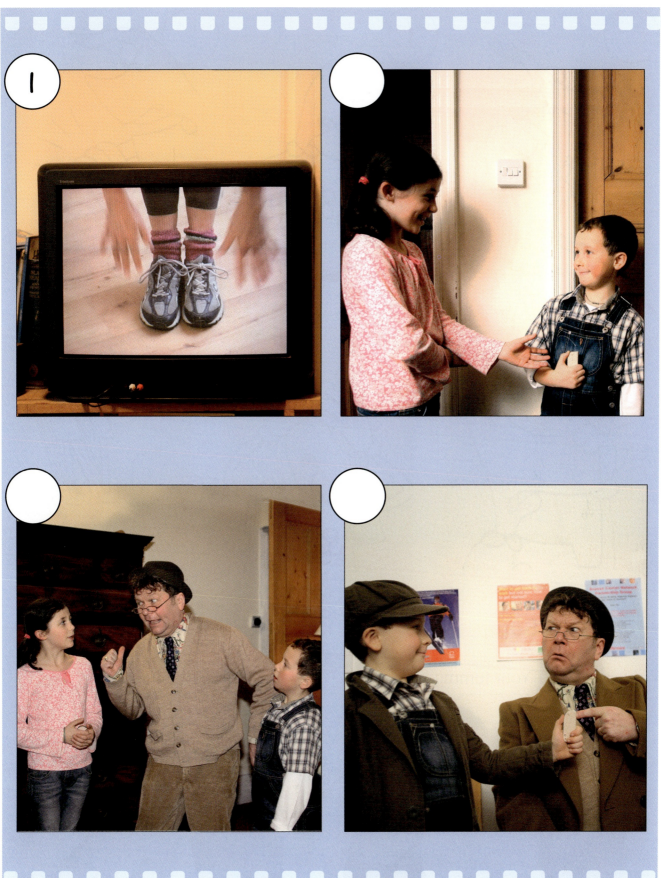

Unit 4

6 **Listen and write the numbers.**

7 **Say.**

Your tummy hurts.

Your shoulder hurts.

My/Your (shoulder) hurts.   My/Your (feet) hurt.   tummy

Unit 4

8 Look and tick (✓).

Units 3-4 — Show what you can do

1 🎵 CD 2, 14 — Listen and write the numbers.

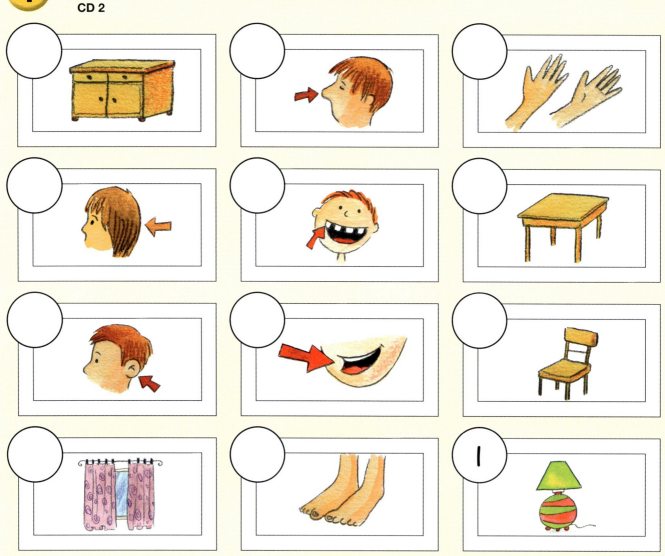

2 Match the words to the pictures.

nose	curtains	1 lamp
chair	hair	tooth
table	ear	mouth
cupboard	hands	feet

Units 3-4

3 Listen and write the numbers.

4 Match the sentences to the pictures.

Let's run!

I can smell onions.

1 My tummy hurts.

Let's watch TV.

31

Unit 5 Clothes

1 Listen and point. (CD 2, 16)

shoes, skirt, woolly hat, jeans, pullover, cap, hat, dress, T-shirt, trainers, jacket, socks

2 Do the sums.

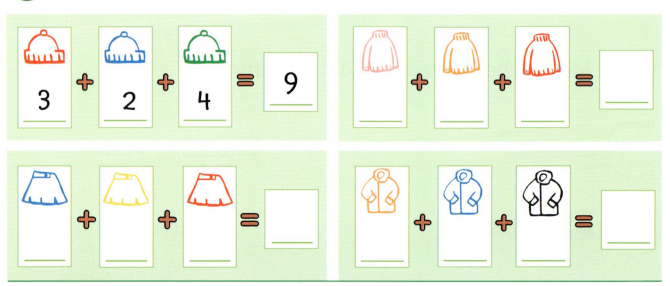

3 + 2 + 4 = 9

pullover woolly hat jeans skirt dress socks jacket trainers T-shirt hat cap shoes

32

3 Listen and point. Write the numbers.

You're in the swimming pool.   Get out of the water.   Dry yourself.   Put on your (shoes).

Unit 5

4   Watch the story. Listen and stick.

(Joe), this (hat) is for you.   I hate it.   Bye-bye!   It's Fred, the fox.   What a lovely hat!   Stupid me!   Wonderful!

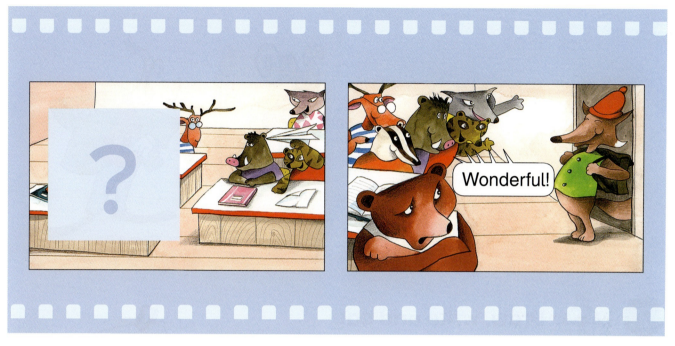

5  **Listen and colour.**

35

Unit 5

6 **Listen and read.**

Look at me

My T-shirt's red.

My jacket's green.

My jeans are blue.

Like a parrot in a zoo.

7 **Draw, write and say.**

Look at me

My  's _____ .

My  's _____ .

My 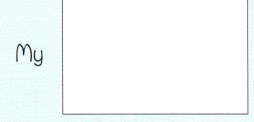 are _____ .

Like a parrot in a zoo.

Look at me.   My (jacket) is (green).   My (jeans) are (blue).

8   Watch the story. Listen and write the numbers.

Unit 6 — Let's count

1   **Listen and point.**

ten · eighty · twenty · fifty · thirty · sixty · ninety · forty · seventy · a hundred

2   **Listen and colour. Say.**

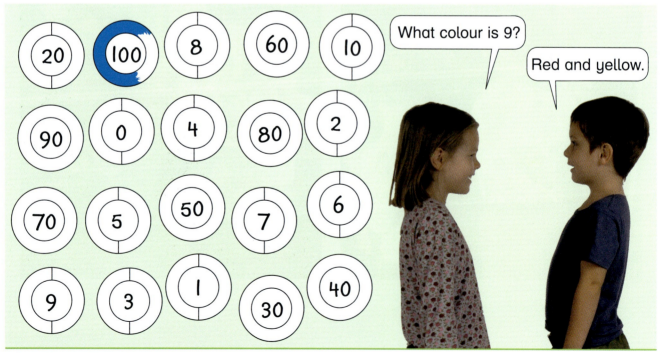

What colour is 9?
Red and yellow.

thirty   forty   fifty   sixty   seventy   eighty   ninety   a/one hundred

Unit 6

3   **Listen and point. Sing the song.**

I've got £10,- £20,- £30,- £40,- £50,- £60,- £70,- £80,- £90,- £100,- in my piggy bank …

Unit 6

 4   Watch the story. Listen and stick.

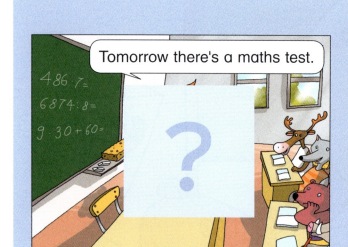
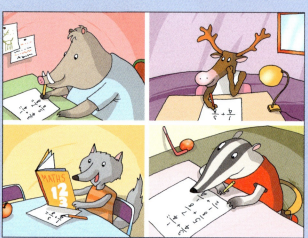

Tomorrow there's a maths test.   I can't do it.   I'm sorry.

Unit 6

5 Play the game. Say.

Throw the dice. I'm/You're the winner.

6 Look and do the sums.

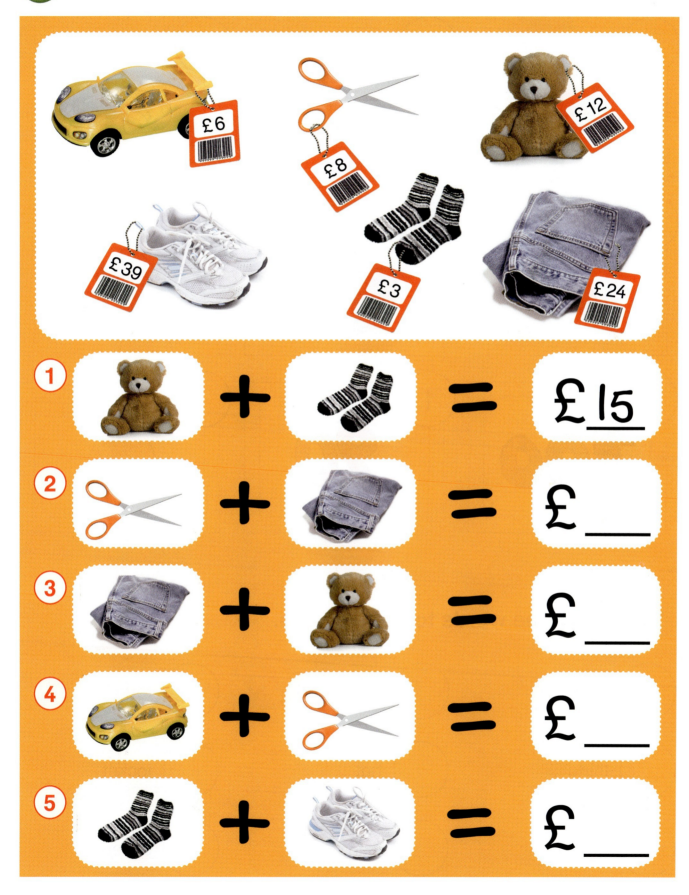

Units 5-6

Show what you can do

1 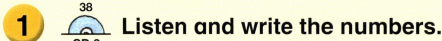 Listen and write the numbers.

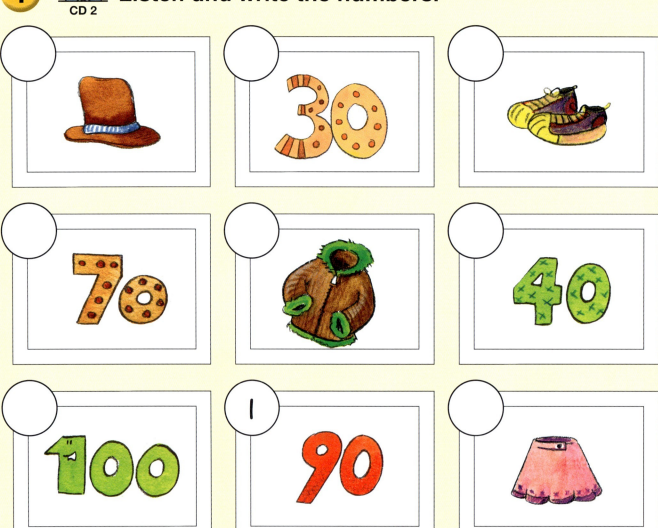

2 Match the words to the pictures.

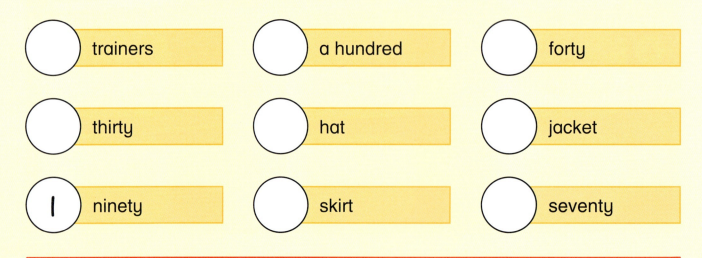

Units 5-6

3 Listen and write the numbers.

1

4 Match the sentences to the pictures.

○ I've got £50 in my piggy bank.

○ I hate it.

○ I can't do it.

1 My cap is green.

45

Unit 7 Family

1 **Listen and write the numbers. Say.**

mum   dad   brother   sister   grandpa   grandma   I think (Tom)'s family is number (one).

2 **Listen and read.**

My mum, my dad, three sisters, two brothers and me. This is my family.

3 **Write. Listen and check.**

My _____ ,
my _____ _____
and me.
This is my _____ .

This is my family.

47

Unit 7

4   Watch the story. Listen and stick.

The racoons are going for a picnic.

Let's go to the river.

Let's help him.

They swim across the river.

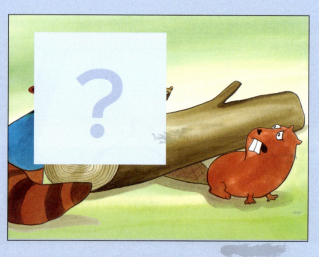

Let's go to the river.   It's a (beaver).   Let's help him.   racoon   I've got an idea.   (The beaver) is very happy.

Unit 7

Unit 7

5   Listen and point. Sing the song.

6 **Listen and point.**

Happy birthday, (Grandpa)!   Do you like (pink roses)?   They smell wonderful.

Unit 8 — On the farm

1 Listen and write the numbers.

cow   sheep   horse   pig   duck   cat   dog   mouse   hen   earthworm

2 Listen and point. Write the numbers.

Call the hens.   Feed the hens.   Look for eggs.   Pick up an egg.   chick

Unit 8

3   Watch the story. Listen and stick.

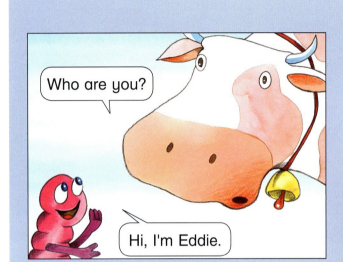
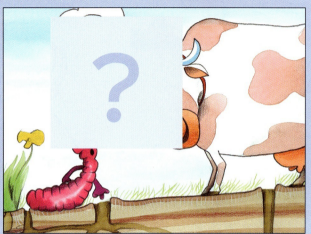

Who are you?

Unit 8

Unit 8

4 14/15 CD 3 **Listen and point. Sing the song.**

Unit 8

5 Match the sentences to the pictures. Write the numbers.

- Snakes, birds, foxes and frogs eat earthworms.
- Very old earthworms are 8 years old.
- Earthworms eat old leaves.
- 1 — Earthworms live underground.
- Earthworms grow to be 9–30 cm long.

Units 7-8

Show what you can do

1 🎧 CD 3 · 16 **Listen and write the numbers.**

2 **Match the words to the pictures.**

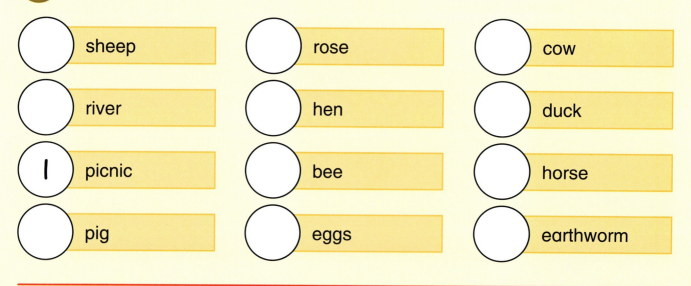

Units
7-8

3   Listen and write the numbers.

◯    ◯

①    ◯

4 Match the sentenses to the pictures.

◯ My sister is very sad.   ① I've got an idea.

 They smell wonderful.   Happy birthday, Anna!

59

Unit 9 Travelling

1 **Listen and point. Say.**

left right

Unit 9

2   Listen and draw lines. Say.

How do you get to school?

 Simon

 Pamela

 Ben

 Maria

 by car

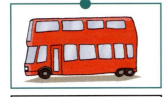 by bus

 I walk

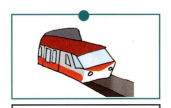 by underground

3 Listen and point. Say the chant.

underground   How do you get to school?   By (bus).   I walk.

61

Unit 9

4   Watch the story. Listen and stick.

What a heavy (basket).   Can we have one?   (Timmy) goes by (bike).

Unit 9

5 25/26 CD 3 **Listen and point. Sing the song.**

6 **Colour and say.**

Unit 9

7 **Listen and say the rhyme.**

First by bike ,

Then by train,

Then by boat ,

And then by plane,

Travelling from six to one,

Travelling, travelling is such fun!

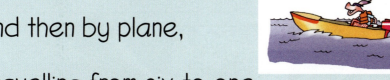

8 **Draw. Create your own poem.**

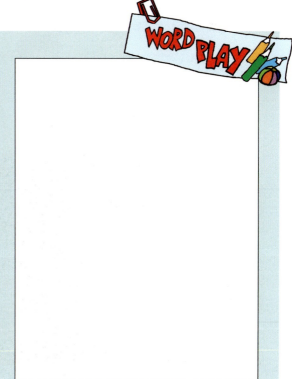

First by _____ ,

Then by train,

Then by _____ ,

And then by plane,

Travelling from six to one,

Travelling, travelling is such fun!

First by (car) and then by (train). (Travelling) is such fun!

65

Unit 10 Holidays

1 Watch the story. Listen and write the numbers.

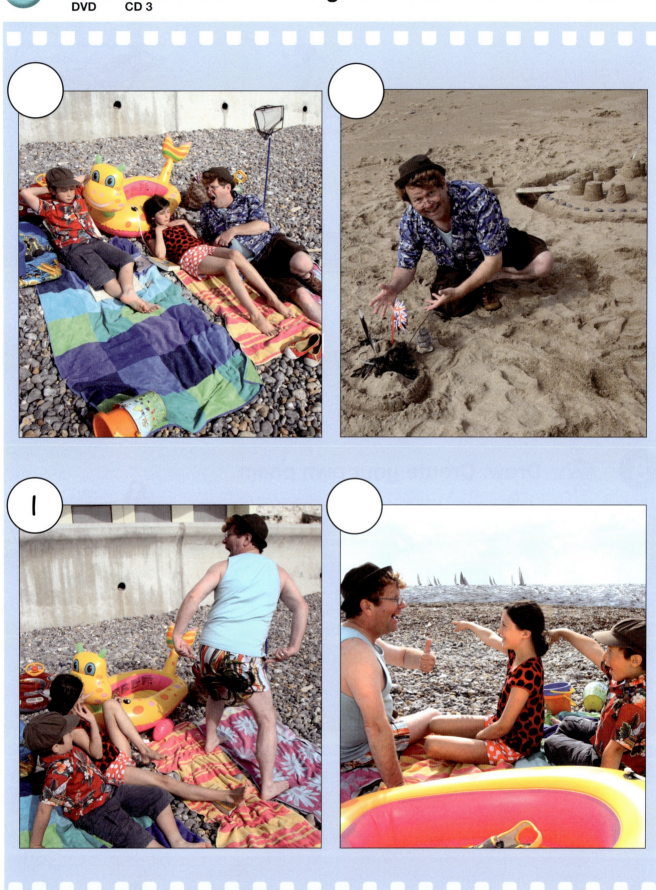

Unit 10

2 Listen and point. Write the numbers.

You're riding your bike. You're hot. You can see (a lake). Cool off Dive into the water.
There's something in your mouth.

Unit 10

3   **Watch the story. Listen and stick.**

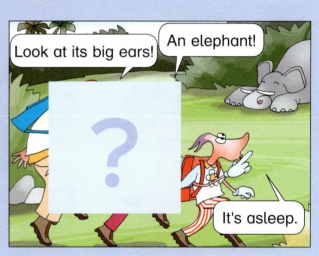

Let's be quiet.   It's asleep.   See you again!

Unit 10

4 36/37 CD 3 **Listen and point. Sing the song.**

Unit 10

5 Read and write the numbers.

1

1) Turtles, fish, sharks and other animals live in the sea. They all need clean water and food.

2) Old bags and bottles make the sea very dirty. Sometimes the animals eat them and get very ill. Don't throw old bottles and bags into the sea.

3) Holidays at the beach are great. People love swimming. They like to make sand castles.

4) 72% of the Earth is water. 28% of the Earth is land.

71

Units 9-10

Show what you can do

1 🎧 **Listen and write the numbers.**
CD 3 · 39

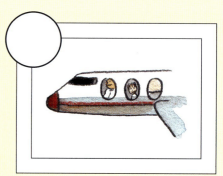

 (1)

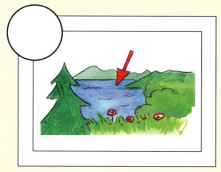

2 **Match the words to the pictures.**

◯ go by train   ◯ lake   ◯ go by underground

(1) boat   ◯ go by bus   ◯ walk

◯ go by bike   ◯ go by plane   ◯ elephant

72

Units 9-10

3 **Listen and write the numbers.**

4 Match the sentences to the pictures.

◯ Tom is asleep.   ◯ Let's be quiet.

◯ What a big snake.   ◯ Bye-bye, see you again.

Picture Dictionary

Unit 1 Hello again

melon

grapes

peach

nuts

kiwi

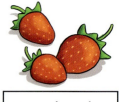
strawberries

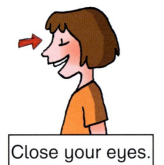
Close your eyes.

Open your mouth.

Unit 2 Shopping

potatoes

tomatoes

carrots

onions

green/red peppers

cucumbers

How much is it?

Unit 3
In my house

sofa

chair

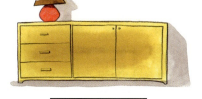
cupboard

curtains

TV

lamp

table

telephone

floor

door

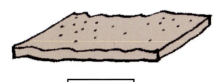
mat

75

Unit 4 My body

eyes

mouth

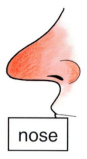

nose

hands

head

ears

hair

shoulders

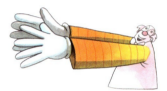

arms

fingers

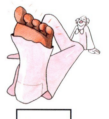

toes

legs

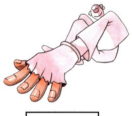

foot/feet

Shake your head.

Clap your hands.

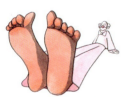

Stamp your feet.

Touch the chair.

My tummy hurts.

shoes

pullover

woolly hat

skirt

socks

jacket

trainers

T-shirt

dress

hat

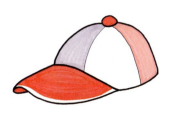
cap

Unit 5
Clothes

Unit 6 Let's count

piggy bank

camera

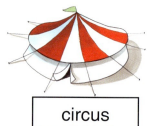
circus

10 ten

20 twenty

30 thirty

forty

fifty

60 sixty

70 seventy

eighty

90 ninety

a hundred

Unit 7 Family

river

sister and brother

dad and mum

grandpa and grandma

78

Unit 8 On the farm

 eggs

 hen

 pig

 cow

 earthworm

 sheep

 horse

 honey

 Who are you?

I live underground.

Unit 9 Travelling

 bus

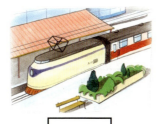 train

 car

 plane

 underground

 Can we have one?

79

Unit 10 Holidays

lake

tiger

jungle

beach

Let's be quiet.

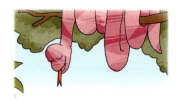
The snake is asleep.

Help me!

Acknowledgements:

The authors and publishers would like to thank the following for permission to reproduce photographs:
Aquili Guiseppe p.61 (t/children); Eichholzer Gerda pp. 7 (children), 15 (children), 24 (children), 28 (children), 38 (children), 46 (b/girl); Fotoliaphoto pp. 29 (senses/Torsten Schon), 43 (toycar/Teamarbeit), 71 (beach/Pupo), 71 (turtle/Hennie Kissling), 71 (shark/Richard Carey); iStockphoto pp. 29 (icecreamgirl/Debi Bishop), 29 (boy with horse/Macatack), 29 (boy listening/marka Wariatka), 29 (girl smelling/yenwen), 29 (boy looking/morganl), 43 (socks/LizV), 43 (price tag/KMITU), 43 (trainers/lostinbids), 43 (scissors/dsafanda), 43 (teddy bear/matmart), 43 (jeans/evemilla), 57 (background earthworm/fishbgone), 57 (leaves/dirkr), 57 (ground/creacart), 57 (soil/ buketbariskan), 57 (blackbird/andyb001), 57 (worms/Antagain), 57 (background/a_Taiga), 71 (map/janrysavy), 71 (polluted water/jphotostyles); 71 (reef/strmko); Charlotte Macpherson Photography, London pp. 5 (Mr Matt), 27 (Mr Matt), 37 (Mr Matt), 66 (Mr Matt); David Tolley p. 46 (family photos)

The authors and publishers are grateful to the following illustrators:
Svjetlan Junaković, Zagreb; Mercè Orti, Barcelona; Antje Hagemann, Berlin; Michael Hülse, Hamburg; Axel Nicolai, Brauweiler; Anke am Berg, Berlin

The publishers are grateful to the following contributors:
Gerda Eichholzer; Charlotte Macpherson: commissioned photography
Andrew Oliver: cover design
Amanda Hockin: concept design
Hansjörg Magerle – Studio HM: book design and page make-up
Bill Ledger: cover illustration

Unit 2
Shopping

Unit 3
In my house

Unit 5
Clothes

Unit 6 Let's count

4
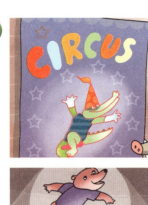   

Unit 7 Family

4

Unit 8 On the farm

3

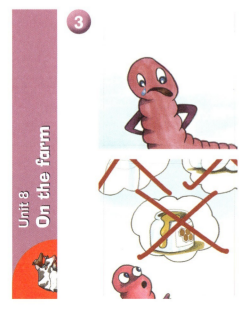